THE PEACE,
NO ARGUMENTS MINDSET

THE PEACE, NO ARGUMENTS MINDSET

And **50 OTHER WAYS** to Achieve Positive Outcomes and Happiness for Your Children and Family

David Solomon

gatekeeper press

Tampa, Florida

THE PEACE, NO ARGUMENTS MINDSET:
And 50 Other Ways to Achieve Positive Outcomes
and Happiness for Your Children and Family

Library of Congress Control Number: 2023947137

ISBN (paperback): 9798988535546
eISBN: 9798988535522

TABLE OF CONTENTS

INTRODUCTION

Peace. You, your children, and your family deserve to enjoy peace and peace of mind. Just thinking about it makes you feel great. However, one of the major obstacles to achieving and enjoying peace with your children is arguments. This book, and the Peace, No Arguments Mindset, will help you prevent and resolve arguments in order to achieve and maintain the many benefits of peace with your children and family, including creating and cherishing wonderful memories.

And there are many times throughout each day, including during discussions and interactions with your children, that can result in negative outcomes, stress, and upset. This book will also help you achieve positive outcomes, decrease stress, and enjoy happiness with your children and family throughout each day.

While the principles and practices are primarily intended for your discussions and interactions with your children, they *also* apply to your spouse, extended family, friends, colleagues, and subordinates (if any).

Avoiding arguments and enjoying peace with your spouse will greatly benefit you, your spouse, *and your children.*

BACKGROUND

My wife Kathleen and I adopted our first daughter from a state Department of Social Services when she was 10 years old. She had suffered years of severe abuse and neglect, with profound negative, emotional consequences, and diagnoses. Our second daughter was 12 years old when we adopted her from the Department of Social Services of a different state. Our daughters are 31 and 27, respectively, at this time. Our first daughter still lives with us.

The book is based on my philosophies, principles, and practices that I have developed, and used and shared with our two daughters. And I have learned a lot about the challenges of parenting from parenting our daughters. These challenges include those "typical" of children growing up and the additional challenges of adopted children with their horrible, pre-adoption histories. In a way, over the years, I feel I have learned a lot about the intricacies of psychology and psychiatry.

SHORT, RIGHT-TO-THE-POINT (BUT NICELY) BOOK FORMAT

A little story....

On Wednesday, November 18, 1863, President Abraham Lincoln traveled to the site of a major battle of the Civil War. He was there to speak at the dedication of the Gettysburg National Cemetery in Gettysburg, Pennsylvania, the next day.

Edward Everett, the most famous orator of the time, gave a speech of approximately 13,000 words during the dedication. The speech was well received by the crowd of about 20,000 people. President Lincoln followed Mr. Everett. The president's speech was only about 272 words.

The next day, in a letter to President Lincoln, Mr. Everett wrote, "I should be glad, if I could flatter myself, that I came as near to the central idea of the occasion in two hours, as you did in two minutes." *https://www.har-vardmagazine.com/2013/11/vita-edward-everett*

This book has, very humbly, something in common with Lincoln's Gettysburg Address. Both his monumental, historic speech and this book have a lot of information and meaning in a short, succinct, and nice right-to-the-point format.

THE BEGINNING ...

As you read this book, I believe you will be thinking and feeling, "This makes sense," and "This will help make a positive difference for me, my children, and my family."

And the first chapter is The Benefits of the Peace, No Arguments Mindset for Your Child and You...

Chapter One

THE BENEFITS OF THE PEACE, NO ARGUMENTS MINDSET FOR YOUR CHILD AND YOU

Part 1: Arguments

Mom or dad angrily says to the child, "You can't talk that way to me!"

What is an all-time leading cause of arguments? Anger. Being angry. That's why we begin with the brief definition of two important words: argument and anger.

DEFINITION OF ARGUMENT

- An angry quarrel or disagreement.
  https://www.merriam-webster.com/dictionary/argument
- A strong and sometimes angry disagreement in talking and discussing something.
  https://dictionary.cambridge.org/us/dictionary/english/argument

- An argument is a conversation in which people disagree with each other angrily or noisily.

  https://www.collinsdictionary.com/us/dictionary/english/argument

DEFINITION OF ANGER (AND ANGRY)

- A strong feeling of displeasure and usually of antagonism (actively expressed opposition or hostility).

  https://www.merriam-webster.com/dictionary/anger

- A strong feeling of displeasure and belligerence aroused by a wrong.

  https://www.dictionary.com/browse/anger

- The feeling people get when something unfair, painful, or bad happens.

  https://dictionary.cambridge.org/us/dictionary/english/anger

- **Anger** is an emotion characterized by antagonism toward someone or something you feel has deliberately done you wrong.

  https://www.apa.org/topics/anger/ (American Psychological Association)

OF COURSE, IT'S NOT PERSONAL

The definitions of "argument" include anger. And the definitions of "anger" or "angry" are based on personal feelings.

Preventing an argument and maintaining peace is based on believing that in any discussion or interaction with your child, nothing that your child says or does is personal, in any way, against you. When you know, "It's not personal," you eliminate a basis for you becoming angry, prevent an argument, and maintain peace.

Obviously, there will always be disagreements with your child. But when you remember that any disagreement is not personal, you will prevent a disagreement from escalating to anger and an argument with your child. Resolving disagreements together without an argument will also set a good example for your child and his interactions with friends, and for later in life.

Even when your child says something inappropriate to you and you say to your child, "You can't talk that way to *me*!" although you say "me!" it's still not personal.

(If it really is personal, that is, your child deliberately and repeatedly tries to cause or causes you emotional or mental trauma [and not just your interpretation of being insulted or disrespected], your child needs a mental health [and medical] evaluation.)

EMOTIONAL STAGES

When it comes to seeing your child's behavior or having a discussion with your child, you can experience positive or negative emotional stages. On the negative side there are stages of frustration, aggravation, upset, and anger. And within each stage there are degrees, before reaching the next stage.

Frustrated, very frustrated, extremely frustrated, then...

Aggravated, very aggravated, extremely aggravated, then...

Upset, very upset, extremely upset, then...

Anger – Angry

If you get angry (or too emotional), while you might think anger gets you motivated to do something about a situation, being angry decreases your focus and decreases your ability to actually do something *correctly* about a situation. (This is in addition to other negative emotional and physical effects of anger.)

Stop and Think

As you progress through the emotional stages, it is critical to Stop and Think.

From relatively small, difficult discussions and situations to major, negative events involving your child, you need all your patience and abilities to focus to resolve the problem.

When faced with a bad/horrible situation involving your child, to be able to think clearly and take the appropriate steps to help your child, you need to decrease or set aside your justified, massive emotional response. Obviously, that is overwhelmingly easier said than done. But being able to first stop and think, as clearly as possible, may make the difference for ultimately having a positive outcome.

You are in charge. Even if you think your child is trying to start an argument, or he really is, it takes two to argue. Don't be provoked. Instead, deescalate. Then determine what is really going on and resolve the problem. (Hopefully, you're not trying to start an argument.)

And remember, "It's not personal."

THE PROS AND CONS OF ARGUING

Is there anything positive or good about an argument? Make a list of the pros and cons:

Pros	Cons
....	....
....	....
....	....
....	....
....	....
....	....

Anything in the Pros column? What possible good can come from having an argument? Is there anything that is accomplished by having an argument that couldn't be accomplished without the argument?

There are only negative consequences of arguments, no positive accomplishments.

There is a long list in the Cons against having arguments (see the rest of the book).

LIMIT IT TO ONE PROBLEM (OR CRISIS) AT A TIME

When there is an issue, problem, trouble, difficulty, or challenge with your child, if you get into an argument while you are trying to resolve the problem, you still have the original problem *plus* the negative consequences of the argument, which may include new problems.

An argument does not solve the underlying, preexisting problem. An argument can or will create new problems.

RECOVERY

Of course, if you have an argument with your child, you both need to recover from the argument, *as effectively and quickly as possible.* It is important for your child to see and feel how you work together to end an argument, fully recover, and make things better, without any long-term harm. Also, it is essential for him to see and feel that things are still loving and great in your relationship.

Recovering from an argument is important and an excellent use of your time. But the goal is always to avoid an escalation to anger and prevent arguments, save time, and make recoveries unnecessary.

Be Slow and Quick

When it comes to anger and arguments, and recovery, are you quick to anger and argue, and slow to recover? Or are you slow to anger and argue, and quick to recover?

Think about the difference. Think about the benefits for you and your child for being slow to anger and argue, and quick to recover. And if there's room for improvement, start today.

Cumulative "Toxicity" of Arguments and The Vicious Cycle: Arguments, Tension, and the Negative Atmosphere in Your Home

There's a term in pharmacology called "cumulative toxicity." This refers to the usual dose of a medication given over time building up in the body to the point where it becomes excessive or toxic, depending on the medication. There are several possible causes of cumulative toxicity, which are not relevant here.

What is relevant is that there is a cumulative toxicity to repeated arguments over days, weeks, months, and years. It gets to a point where you and your child are either having an argument or you're dreading the next argument.

Arguments, on their own, regardless of their basis, increase stress and tension for everyone (including pets) in your home.

The greater the number and more severe the arguments, the greater the tension. And then the greater the tension, the more arguments. It's a vicious, negative cycle.

As the total number of arguments, the duration of each argument, and the severity of each argument all increase, the cumulative toxic effect has increased detrimental effects for your child (and you). These adverse effects include changing his personality, his ability to interact with others (peers and adults), and his health (related to stress and a decreased quality and quantity of sleep). All these changes are for the worse. These traumatic effects can be both short term and long term. Your child is always dreading the next argument.

Your child's home life gets to the point that he can't wait to go to his room, or until it's bedtime and go to sleep. However, then there is probably a decreased quality of sleep. And possibly a decreased duration or interruption of sleep. When he wakes up there is a dread of more arguments that day. The decreased quality and quantity of sleep can adversely affect his health, thinking, and school performance. And make him irritable, which may contribute to the negative cycle.

If you think the cumulative toxic effects described are exaggerated, think how you would have felt, or did feel, at his age and over time.

CONSEQUENCES

Arguments, especially arguments with your child, have many negative consequences and harmful effects, including increased anxiety and setting a negative tone for future discussions.

Avoiding arguments, therefore, have many positive consequences and benefits, including the most important benefit of no arguments: peace.

Part 2: **The Benefits of The Peace, No Arguments Mindset...**

THE BENEFITS OF THE PEACE, NO ARGUMENTS MINDSET FOR YOUR CHILD

Decreased Stress and Peace

With peace there is a positive, happy cycle. When there are no arguments, that decreases stress, which increases happiness, which decreases arguments, which decreases stress, which increases happiness, and so on.

Your child enjoys a more pleasant environment and daily home life, not worrying about the next argument or experiencing the next argument.

Your child knows that when he has a problem, he can always come to you without worrying about getting into an argument, in addition to struggling with his problem. He will come to you sooner, which will prevent a small problem from getting bigger, and a big problem from becoming a crisis.

Better sleep (quality and quantity) and better health.

Improved interactions, less arguing, with his siblings. That's wonderful for everyone.

Peace of Mind.

The Memories

Thirty years from now, forty years from now, and for the rest of his life, you want your child to have wonderful, positive memories of his childhood.

You don't want "We were constantly arguing," "All we did was argue," or "There was one argument after another argument," to be the most prominent memories of his childhood.

Positive memories of peace during his childhood will help him in raising his children in a peaceful family.

THE BENEFITS OF THE PEACE, NO ARGUMENTS MINDSET FOR YOU

Decreased Stress and Peace

You enjoy a more pleasant daily home life, not having to worry about the next argument or experiencing the argument.

With peace there is a positive, happy cycle. When there are no arguments, that decreases stress, which increases happiness, which decreases arguments, which decreases stress, which increases happiness, and so on.

Better sleep (quality and quantity) and better health.

Peace of Mind.

As you can see, peace has the same benefits for your child and you.

Perhaps you think that an argument is a form of "blowing off steam." There are less combative and more productive ways to decrease anger and stress. Stop and think what works best for you to avoid escalation to anger and an argument. And you will know for future situations how to avoid anger and an argument in the early stage of a discussion.

Save Precious Time

Important: Time – the moments you have with your child – is the most cherished thing you and your family have together. Time is more precious than money, gold, jewels, and any of the other so-called "valuables." Time is finite and you don't know how much of it you have.

You don't know when you or your child may have an accident or get a bad diagnosis that will tragically decrease the quality and quantity of the precious time you have together as a family. Then it's too late to think, "I wish I/we had not wasted all of those hours and days arguing."

Do a study: Keep a log of the time spent arguing and recovering from an argument. Perhaps you don't realize how much time you spend arguing and then recovering from the arguments.

Again, what positive outcome is achieved with an argument that couldn't have been accomplished without an argument? In less time. And you still have the original situation, topic, or problem to address and resolve, which takes more cherished time!

Arguments are an incredible waste of precious, precious time. You can never get that wasted time back or have it replaced.

The Memories

If your childhood memories are good and positive, then you know how important that is for you and how important good memories will be for your child.

If your childhood memories are bad and negative, then you know how sad that is and how important it is to prevent bad memories and make sure you make good, positive memories for your child.

It's comforting for you, and you feel better knowing you are improving your child's present, daily life and his future, including wonderful memories of his childhood. And he will want to provide good memories for his children (your grandchildren)!

Life is all about the memories: enjoying creating great memories and enjoying and cherishing looking back on the great memories.

THE PEACE, NO ARGUMENTS MINDSET.
MINDSET VS. MOOD

Definition of Mindset

- A fixed mental attitude or disposition that predetermines a person's responses to and interpretations of situations.

  Mindset - definition of mindset by The Free Dictionary

- A habitual or characteristic mental attitude that determines how you will interpret and respond to situations.

  Mindset - Definition, Meaning & Synonyms | Vocabulary.com

- A mental attitude or inclination. A fixed state of mind.

  Mind-set Definition & Meaning - Merriam-Webster

It is important that The Peace, No Arguments philosophies and priorities become a mindset, The Peace, No Arguments Mindset, and not subject to your mood or the events of the day, which can vary for many reasons.

You and your family will experience the benefit of having a Peace, No Arguments Mindset on the first day. And as the Peace positive cycle develops and continues, the benefits to your family will continue and increase.

. Chapter Two .

ACHIEVING AND ENJOYING POSITIVE, PEACEFUL DISCUSSIONS WITH YOUR CHILD

Tone

Of tone, setting and distance, volume, and body language, the tone of your voice is the most important and influential asset you possess to insure a positive outcome from a discussion or any verbal interaction with your child.

HOW TO MAKE A POSITIVE DIFFERENCE WITH A POSITIVE TONE OF VOICE

The tone of your voice should always be sincerely positive, providing steadiness and reassurance, especially during a difficult discussion.

The tone should be essentially flat, within a narrow range, ending a sentence on an up note or down note, as needed.

Your tone should be positive or neutral, never negative. What you are saying, the content, may be negative, as in opposing what your child has said or done, but your content should be expressed with a positive tone.

To convey a sincere, positive tone you must *sincerely believe* in the benefits of a positive tone and what you want to achieve. This is in addition to sincerely believing in what you are saying, of course.

A positive tone of voice will enhance and support the content of what you are saying. A negative tone of voice will change, distract, and detract from the content of what you are saying.

You can say the exact same words with a different tone of voice and change the meaning, message, effect, and outcome of the words and conversation. The same words will have a different meaning and outcome, based only on a different tone.

The tone at the end of the sentence is especially important. The tone may be uplifting, reassuring, or encouraging, or a lower, calming tone at the end of the sentence, as appropriate for the discussion and goal.

Tone, in this section, does not refer to emphasizing individual words, which can also be useful and change the meaning of a sentence. Emphasizing individual words (including with a pause after the word or repeating the word) is critical to make certain points and avoid misunderstandings.

A positive, *reassuring* tone of voice (combined with reassuring body language) lets your child know that he can count on you, even when the child has said or done something negative or wrong. And when you consistently use a positive, reassuring tone of voice in many discussions, despite how negative your child's behavior, he will have increased confidence that he can come to you with a problem or concern.

Examples of a negative tone of voice: aggressive, antagonistic, argumentative, baiting, belligerent, challenging, confrontational, hostile, impatient, intimidating, provocative, sarcastic, and taunting.

A positive tone of voice helps insure a positive outcome for a discussion. A negative tone of voice probably results in a negative outcome. Be positive.

TONE AND CONTENT

When you have bad news, your tone of voice cannot change the facts of what you are saying, the content; but a positive (as much as possible), appropriate tone can help change your child's *reaction* to the content.

EMERGENCY

As always when the safety or health, especially the immediate safety or health of your child or you are at risk or of concern, then an Emergency, Urgent, Grave or similar tone of voice (and volume and body language) is necessary.

When your Emergency or similar tone of voice is used only for emergency situations, your child will know the situation is really an emergency (vs. you having an angry tone reacting to a non-emergency situation).

A LITTLE STORY

My wife, first daughter, and I were asked to do a public service video, including a voice-over, to promote adoption of children through the state. I was focused. I had one line for the voice-over. The line was something like, "I think I'm ready to adopt a child at this time." Beginner's luck. The director told me that my first try was great. But he wanted a second try, and this time smile while speaking the line. The lesson: A sincere smile always helps the tone of your voice and your message.

REPEAT

Of tone, setting and distance, body language, and volume, the tone of your voice is the most important and influential asset you possess to insure a positive outcome from a discussion or interaction with your child.

Setting and Distance

The setting and distance between you and your child for a discussion are important for a positive outcome.

SETTING

When possible, plan for the setting, especially for important topics of discussion. Of course, there are times when your child comes to you and starts a discussion, and you can't choose the setting.

HOME

Neutral and Non-threatening
In a planned discussion, the setting should be neutral and non-threatening, such as the living room, kitchen, or dining area. Your child's bedroom can provide comfort and reassurance. Your study, office, or bedroom is usually not as comfortable and not as appropriate, unless the situation is urgent.

Also in a planned discussion, you don't want to condition your child to having a discussion in the same place every time, which could increase anxiety. Always asking the child to come to a particular place could trigger his thoughts of a problem and worry, just the opposite of your goal.

If your child comes to you and begins a discussion of an important topic, be patient, and, if possible, direct your child to the best setting. The more important the topic, the more important the setting.

Lighting

The lighting should not be too bright, that's distracting, and not too dark, that's depressing, ominous, and dampens the mood.

Sound

Pleasant, calming music at an appropriate volume is ideal for a discussion with your child. If certain music is known to be calming or a positive influence, as in associated with a positive memory, it is worth taking the time, if not too complicated, to put on or turn up the positive music. This applies only if taking the time for the music does not interfere with the discussion.

You don't want a noisy setting or distracting music, especially music associated with negative memories.

Background

The background or setting should be comfortable and positive; and not distracting or too serious (e.g., pictures of relatives who have passed away) for the discussion.

(For negotiating with or selling something to someone, you want your back to, for example, a window with beautiful scenery outside or a similar background. This provides the other person with the "wonderful view" as a positive "distraction" and puts the individual/customer more at ease and in a favorable mood. You do not want the background to be a negative distraction or detract from the discussion.)

Seated

When you can, as in a planned discussion, or nicely interrupt a discussion, and have you and your child sit down comfortably.

OUT OF THE HOUSE

When you and your child are out of your home, and the need arises for a discussion, your options for an ideal setting are limited. The most important consideration is for a quiet place with few or no distractions.

NOT HUNGRY

It does not fit in the usual definition of setting, but whenever possible you do not want to have your child hungry at the time of a discussion.

Sometimes when you are hungry you get grumpy, distracted, or both. You don't want to have a discussion with your child, especially a serious or upsetting discussion, when he is grumpy or distracted. If possible, when your child is hungry, wait until at least he has a snack before a conversation. That will help achieve the proper "setting" for a discussion.

DISTANCE

Goldie Locks …. Just Right
Sitting about three to five feet apart is best.

Don't be too far apart. If you are too far apart, there is a decreased or essentially no connection. And both individuals strain to hear and wrongly increase the volume of their voices. Or you or your child misunderstand information. Undesirable.

Don't be too close. If you are too close, that could be intimidating and possibly "threatening," which would detract from the topic and the goal of the discussion. The closer you are to your child, the more threatening, especially if you have an index finger pointed at him.

You can adjust *your* distance, rather than asking your child to adjust his distance.

You should lean back or sit up straight. Do not lean forward unless you are kindly emphasizing a point. By leaning forward, you express an important point and a more sincere feeling.

For height, try to be on the same level as your child, not higher than the child. A little lower is okay. The appropriate height is more reassuring, and less or not threatening. Do not stand over your child.

EMERGENCY

Of course, when the safety and health, especially the immediate safety and health, of you and/or your child is at risk or of concern, that requires an immediate, emergency or urgent statement or discussion, regardless of the setting or distance!

Volume

During a discussion with your child, the appropriate volume (sound level of your voices) will help avoid problems and achieve a positive outcome.

SOFT AND LOW

Use a soft, low voice (low volume) to open and continue throughout a discussion with your child. Speak consistently soft and low, even (and especially) if your child raises his voice.

Negative: If *you* increase your volume, especially first, then your child is likely to *react* and increase his volume.

Negative example: Your child starts to increase his volume. You: "Stop raising your voice." Him: "I'm not raising my voice!" You: "You Are Raising Your Voice." Him: "No, I'm Not Raising My Voice!!" You: "Yes, You Are Raising Your Voice!" Him: "No, I'm NOT Raising My Voice!!!"

Positive: You should always maintain your low volume or progressively decrease your volume. The more your child raises his voice, the more you lower your voice, subtly and slowly.

Positive example: Your child starts to increase his volume. Calmly and quietly say, "Please speak softer." …. Repeat if needed. If necessary, say, "Please speak your softest."

Positive example: Your child starts to increase his volume. In a nice, low voice with a reassuring tone, say, "I can hear you, no problem, no need to raise your voice; please speak softer."

It takes two raised voices for a discussion to escalate to an argument, and then to a fight. The first person raises the volume, then the other, then the first raises the volume even greater. Rapid escalation. Avoid escalation by keeping your voice soft and low. *You* can control the volume of *your* voice.

Increased volume during the discussion distracts and detracts from the topic and goal of the discussion.

Avoid using a volume that is too low, to the point where your child can't clearly understand you. That would be frustrating for your child, decrease or prevent effective communication, and increase the chance of miscommunication (possibly resulting in a future argument).

The appropriate volume depends on the appropriate distance (see Setting and Distance) from your child.

AVOID REACTING

Your child may increase his volume specifically to get a reaction. Don't react. Don't raise your voice. Of course, that's easier said than done. Focus on the priority and the goal of the discussion.

After a few discussions with your child increasing his volume and you not reacting and not increasing your volume and you not getting angry, your child will decrease his volume and discontinue the practice.

THE FUTURE

You are setting an important example for your child that he will remember (*memories!*) and benefit from in all future relationships, including in work, with his future spouse and children, and with friends and colleagues.

EMERGENCY

By always using a low volume for discussions, you set an expectation for you and your child. And when you increase your volume, with an emergency or urgent tone and message, your child knows the situation is an emergency or urgent!

When the safety and health of you and/or your child, especially the immediate safety and health of you or your child, is at risk or of concern, then you need the Emergency or Urgent *increased* volume for strong emphasis and absolute clarity of your communication and emergency message.

Body Language

We start with the basic definition of body language.

DEFINITION

- The movements or positions of your body that show other people how you are feeling, without using words.

  https://dictionary.cambridge.org/us/dictionary/english/body-language

- The gestures, movements, and mannerisms by which a person or animal communicates with others.

  https://www.merriam-webster.com/dictionary/body%20language

- The nonverbal imparting of information by means of conscious or subconscious bodily gestures, posture, etc.

  https://www.collinsdictionary.com/us/dictionary/english/body-language

An important point is that body language may be intentional or unintentional. By being aware of your body language, you can use it intentionally to help positively communicate with your child. In addition, you can consciously avoid unintentional, negative body language, which sends negative messages.

Since there are two people, you and your child, having the discussion, there are two sets of body language.

YOU

Facial Expression

Of course, the first and most important part of your body language is your facial expression, which should be used to reinforce what you are saying, your message.

Your facial expression should be generally nice and re-assuring, not upset, even when there is reason to be upset. Have a pleasant expression and smile when appropriate, not a grin.

Your facial expression should be a positive one to support and enhance your message.

Your facial expression should not be a negative one, which would distract and detract from your message and the focus of the discussion. Your negative facial expression would become a negative message on its own, no matter what the topic being discussed.

A new proverb: A negative facial expression, including rolling your eyes, is worth a thousand insults to your child.

Other Body Language

Avoid intimidating and confrontational movements and actions, such as finger pointing and making a fist (obviously not a threatening fist, but just a clenched hand). This is especially important to avoid if the intimidating movements are accompanied by increased volume and negative tone of voice (also avoid). Such "confrontational" body language leads to confrontations, which are totally avoidable.

Sit back, relaxed, at ease. This helps your child relax and be at ease, especially, and even when, he starts out upset or nervous.

Don't sit leaning forward constantly, which could be intimidating. Only lean forward (slowly) when nicely supporting or making an especially important, positive point.

Always remember: Your child is seeing or observing, considering, and reacting to your body language, even if he doesn't specifically think about it or know it has the formal name "body language." You need to maintain and exhibit positive body language. You don't want your body language, especially negative body language, to negatively influence your child and his interactions.

YOUR CHILD

Definition of Observe

- To watch carefully, especially with attention to details or behavior for the purpose of arriving at a judgment.

  https://www.merriam-webster.com/dictionary/observe

- To regard with attention, especially so as to see or learn something.

  https://www.dictionary.com/browse/observe

Observe your child's body language, head to toe. Be a "good observer." This is the visual equivalent of being a good listener. It's a lot more than just looking at your child.

For example, is your child fidgeting, not sitting reasonably still? You should compare this behavior or movement to the usual or normal baseline for your child.

The classic: Does your child appear nervous or worried? Also, is the body language indicating increased anxiety or apprehension as the discussion continues and gets into more depth and details?

Match?

Does your child's body language match what he is saying? Or does the mismatch or contradiction indicate he is lying?

Observe the head movement, as in nodding or shaking of the head.   Does the nodding or shaking of the head agree with what he is saying? Especially when observing older children (and adults).

Example: The child says, "Yes, I really did go to the library like you wanted me to"; while he is shaking his head, as in "no, I didn't go to the library." Mismatching of words and head movement can be a subconscious signal of the truth, and indicate he is lying.

Example: The child says, "No, I didn't go over to Joe's this afternoon instead of going to the library"; while he is nodding his head, as in "yes, I did go over to Joe's." Again, mismatching of words and head movement can be a sub-conscious signal of the truth, and indicate he is lying.

Lying Facial Expression

Does your child have a "lying facial expression"? The "lying facial expression" of an individual is based on his known history. Perhaps there is a characteristic change in the facial muscles, such as of the forehead, the eyes, and the lips, to a different, but characteristic, expression. In addition, the child may begin to rock or fidget while sitting, when pre-viously sitting basically still. Or he was looking directly in your eyes during the discussion and now there is a change and he can only look away.

The recognizable "lying facial expression" for your child is an individual reaction, confirmed based on what the child is saying and your knowledge of the current known facts and circumstances, just as you knew he lied and had a similar expression on previous occasions.

The "lying facial expression" is consistent and you have observed it and confirmed it several times in the past.

If you believe you have reasonable certainty that what your child is saying is a lie or extremely likely a lie, his lying facial expression may confirm your beliefs.

The *absence* of the "lying facial expression" *may* (or may not) indicate that, despite when you think your child is lying, he may be telling the truth. Also, the absence of this distinctive body language may indicate that your child was genuinely mistaken about something and not lying about it; when you think he is lying. Therefore, you being open-minded and recognizing the absence of the "lying facial expression" is important in determining the truth.

Changes and Trends

Observe *changes*, whether your child's body language is improving or deteriorating, during the conversation.

Observe *trends* during the conversation. Is there slow, steady improvement or deterioration in your child's body language? For instance, as the conversation continues is he becoming more relaxed and beginning to smile? Or was he previously smiling and now he appears increasingly upset or sad.

A decline in your child's body language may indicate that there is much more going on with him than you are aware of. What your child is saying with his body language may precede or substitute for and speak louder than his verbal language.

Abrupt Change

Critical: Is there an *abrupt negative change* or decline in your child's body language? The discussion may have unintentionally triggered a totally unrelated memory or thought that is very upsetting for him.

This negative change may only be apparent in his body language and not in what your child is saying, at least not yet.

You don't want to misinterpret the abrupt negative change in his body language as necessarily being related to the current topic of discussion.

You don't know everything that has happened to your child that day, or a week ago, or a month ago, or in the distant past that was upsetting at that time and is brought back to his mind by the current discussion.

(The possibility of an abrupt negative change in body language is especially true for foster or adopted children. This is related to trauma experienced by your child before foster care or adoption, and unknown to you.)

You may need to immediately address the newly discovered apparent problem, which is far more important than the original topic of discussion. In this case, when your child starts talking, you stop talking and *listen*.

General Examples of Opposites

Slouching (not attentive) or sitting up relatively straight (attentive).

Arms folded (impatient or upset) or arms behind his head (relaxed).

Leaning forward (paying attention) and leaning back (relaxed *and* paying attention).

Eyes focused on the person you are speaking with, with consistent eye contact (paying attention) or eyes wandering (not paying attention or, if occasionally wandering, thinking of what to say next) or eyes rolling (bad body language).

Know your child. For example, you know that he doesn't have to have constant eye contact to hear and understand what you are saying.

Remember: For your child, wandering eyes could mean that the topic of the conversation is too difficult or upsetting to talk about (and you may or may not know the reason why), or he is lying.

BODY LANGUAGE AND VERBAL LANGUAGE

Body language can be as important or more important, and say more, than verbal language. So, you must be a good observer (a good "listener") for body language.

Content – What You are Saying
for Discussions

INDIVIDUALLY APPROPRIATE

Of course, use age and individual appropriate words during a discussion with your child. A child's chronological age doesn't always reflect his ability to comprehend and process what you are saying. Naturally, you know your child best.

It is critically important to consider your child's known history. Certain words or phrases, not even derogatory words, may trigger a negative memory of a previous negative experience that you are aware of. Avoid those negative trigger words and phrases.

In addition, you may not be aware of other, including more recent, negative experiences for your child. Something bad may have happened at school, with a friend, in a store or anywhere, and your child did not tell you.

If you say something and your child seems to overreact or react much differently than you would expect, then you need to know why your child reacted the way he did, refocus the discussion to find out, and be a good listener.

EFFECTIVE COMMUNICATION

Definition of Communication

- The imparting or interchange of thoughts, opinions, or information by speech, writing, or signs.

  https://www.dictionary.com/browse/communication

- A process by which information is exchanged between individuals through a common system of symbols, signs, or behavior.

  Communication Definition & Meaning - Merri-am-Webster

What's missing from these dictionary definitions is the recipient of the information, your child, understanding the information. It's the second part of communication, the understanding, that makes it *effective* communication. There are techniques you can use to ensure clear, effective communication.

KEEP YOUR MOUTH CLOSED

Mouth Closed and Ears Open

During a difficult discussion with your child, one of the hardest things to do is to *not* say anything.

When the discussion is difficult, the natural "reflex" is to react, respond, open your mouth, and say something. That's easy. It's hard to keep your mouth closed, listen, think about what your child is saying and why he's saying it, and then think about what you should say; before just saying something.

You will find that you have more positive outcomes from discussions when you say less. It's the quality and the timing, not the quantity of your words that's important for successful outcomes.

The Old Saying

The old saying: "If you don't have something nice to say, don't say anything."

The basis for the old saying: What's the point of saying something that's not nice? Why would you say something that's not nice? There's always a reason, but not always a nice reason.

Updated old saying: "If you don't have something nice to say, please keep your mouth closed and listen."

FIRST AND LAST WORDS

Introduce the subject of a sentence or paragraph. The first words you say in a discussion, sentence, or paragraph and the last words you say in a discussion, sentence, or para-graph should be the most important words and informa-tion.

The first words you speak let your child know what to focus on and sets the tone for a discussion.

The last words you speak reinforce the most import-ant point(s) of the discussion and will be the information he is most likely to remember.

EMPHASIS

Emphasizing important words during a discussion with your child will help those words and the information stand out and be remembered, and avoid misunderstandings and arguments.

You can emphasize a certain word or short phrase by pausing before and/or after the word or short phrase, using a slightly different pronunciation of the word, or repeating the word or short phrase.

Pause for Emphasis
Example:

I will meet you at Hobby Lobby, at the entrance, at 4:00.

I will meet you at Hobby Lobby, at the entrance, at... 4:00.

Avoid misunderstandings... and prevent arguments.

Repeat a Word or Phrase for Emphasis

During a discussion, repeat an important word, phrase, or point for emphasis, and your child's memory.

If you make a misstatement or say a wrong word, correct yourself and repeat the correct phrase or word, for clarity and to avoid a misunderstanding (which could lead to an argument).

Combining Pause for Emphasis and Repeat a Word or Phrase for Emphasis

I will meet you at Hobby Lobby, at the entrance, at... 4:00. That's 4:00.

WHEN INFORMATION IS IMPORTANT, SAY IT'S IMPORTANT

Preface telling your child about important information, or the most important information, by saying, "This is important." This will get or increase your child's attention and help him focus on and remember the most important part of the discussion.

HAVE YOUR CHILD (AND YOU) REPEAT BACK IMPORTANT INFORMATION

After you have had a discussion with your child and come up with a plan, have your child repeat back any important general information and the specific plan. This will identify any misunderstandings or errors that need clarification or correction. Then have him repeat back the information and plan again.

After your child has spoken, then you repeat all the information back to your child. This assures both of you that each of you know the plan and sets a good example for your child.

EUPHEMISM

Definition

- The substitution of an agreeable or inoffensive expression for one that may offend or suggest something unpleasant.

  https://www.merriam-webster.com/dictionary/ euphemism

- The substitution of a mild, indirect, or vague expression for one thought to be offensive, harsh, or blunt.

  Euphemism Definition & Meaning | Dictionary.com

Challenges (humorous) vs. Chores. The secret is for your child to feel good when he has completed or accomplished his challenge. It's more than a game, but that's okay too.

Using a euphemism makes a big challenge seem smaller, and easier to accomplish.

DO NOT USE DEROGATORY OR DEMEANING WORDS

In any discussion with your child, never use negative, derogatory, or demeaning words or obscenities, in any form (nouns, verbs, adjectives and adverbs). Negative terms distract and detract from the focus and the important topic of the discussion. Derogatory words make the derogatory words the focus of the discussion and may start an argument.

Avoiding negative words especially applies to avoiding demeaning words about your child himself (or friends) and anything your child is doing, wearing, planning, etc. You can make the same important points about your child's inappropriate behavior, more effectively, without using derogatory or demeaning words.

For example, you nicely say that his choice of clothing is bad (without the negative words), not that he is bad.

And, rather than telling him why you think his clothing is inappropriate, you ask *him* why he chose those clothes. This makes him think about his selection and, hopefully, he realizes that the clothes are inappropriate. At least you now know what he is thinking, and you can address his specific points, without demeaning words.

Negative words or phrases may trigger bad or traumatic memories for your child, including his negative response to the same derogatory words that were used in the past. There may not always be an obvious or even a direct link to your child's bad memory. There can be an unintended, unknown, negative connection. The human brain works very quickly and often seems to go down a negative thought path, especially with related negative past experiences.

Always set a positive example, which will have short-term and long-term benefits, as well as create positive memories.

FOCUS ON ONE TOPIC AT A TIME

Prioritize. Always focus on one topic at a time during a discussion.

For a discussion about a difficult problem or topic, always start with something genuinely and sincerely positive. This sets the best possible tone for the conversation about a difficult problem. Before any negative, have a positive.

If a negative thought or information related to your child comes up during a discussion, that is not directly related to the topic of the discussion, hold the negative thought. You can address the new, negative information after the current problem is resolved. Of course, if the new information is urgent that takes immediate priority.

ASK QUESTIONS

When there is a difficult situation and your child wants to do something you know is not appropriate and do not approve of, sometimes it is best to let your child come to the correct conclusion or plan on his own, by asking him a question.

Rather than reacting and telling your child your thoughts (e.g., that what he wants to do is inappropriate or bad) or telling him what to do, you can ask a question. You ask a non-threatening, one-word question, "Why?"

For an action he is talking about taking; you simply say, "Why?" or "Why do you want to do XYZ?"

For something he said that you disagree with; you say, "Why do you say that?" Or "What do you base that/it on?"

By asking "Why?" you turn things around and have him think about what he is saying or what he wants to do. He may not have thought things through to begin with. Hopefully, your child will realize on his own that his request or statement doesn't make sense, which is better than you telling him that his idea doesn't make sense. If he can't justify things in his own mind, he will come to the correct conclusion.

You can always provide your parental love, wisdom, and guidance at any time.

The "ask questions" approach helps your child learn to think things through *before* asking you.

Also, by asking "Why?" when he gives you his reasons you have learned a lot of information. You can then respond in a specific way to specific information, rather than giving him a flat "no."

AFFIRMATIVE OR POSITIVE SENTENCES OR PHRASES ARE BETTER THAN NEGATIVE SENTENCES

This is a little tricky...

The affirmative form of a phrase is a clearer and more informative way to express information for your child (and adults).

For example...

Negative form: The science project is not going to be easy.

Affirmative form: The science project is going to be extremely difficult.

The affirmative form gives your child more information. In the negative form, your child knows the project is not going to be easy, but he does not know if the project is going to be difficult (neutral), somewhat difficult, moderately difficult, or extremely difficult.

When you use the word "not" the listener knows what something is "not," but may not know what that something is.

Exceptions

There are times when using the negative form, "not," is best. When you want to avoid overwhelming your child with specific information or you want to minimize some task (with a humorous tone) using the non-specific "not" may be the best approach.

AVOID PRONOUNS AND NONSPECIFIC WORDS

Avoid misunderstandings, frustration, and arguments by avoiding pronouns, such as he, she, his, her, it, they, these, those, this, that, and nonspecific words, such as thing and stuff.

Be Specific, especially when you are talking about two or more people, or two or more things. Use the name of the person or persons you are speaking about or name the specific object. Don't rely on the listener being an English major to determine which pronoun is the subject or the object of the sentence. Even if you are redundant with a person's name, it's better than having a misunderstanding.

THREAT

Definition

- A declaration of an intention or determination to inflict punishment, injury, etc., in retaliation for, or conditionally upon, some action or course.

  https://www.dictionary.com/browse/threat?s=t

- A suggestion that something unpleasant or violent will happen, especially if a particular action or order is not followed.

  THREAT | definition in the Cambridge English Dictionary

Of the above definitions the key word for your child is "unpleasant." The unpleasant effect can be either you doing or not doing something that your child wants, taking away something that the child has, or adding a condition to an agreement.

Threats can be actual and literal, or a perception. The threat is in the perception by your child, even if you did not mean what you said to be a threat.

Your words can be felt by your child as a threat in the context of previous discussions and threats. History and memories can make a big negative difference in the perception of a current threat.

Threats can be small or large, as in the threat of taking away something small or large from your child. Something that may seem small to you may be really big and important to your child. Or you may realize something is important, but not realize just how important.

If / Then and When

Turn a threat into a reward. The if/then phrasing, such as if you do this, then something unpleasant will happen, is a threat. But the same situation can be turned around with phrasing as a reward.

And for further emphasis of the reward approach, you can substitute "when" for "if." When you do this, then something pleasant will happen is a reward statement.

BE PATIENT AND OUTCOME ORIENTED

Be patient, positive, and outcome oriented. The out-come-oriented approach becomes the usual positive process and practice.

Nothing (except immediate safety and immediate health) is black and white. Work through issues and dis-agreements, large and small, and achieve the desired outcome.

Don't have absolutes. Absolutes, such as you say, "You will do this," to your child is frequently the first sentence of an argument, especially if you use an argumentative tone. Avoid an argument. The desired *outcome* is the priority.

This approach is *not* "negotiating" with your child, which you might consider inappropriate. This approach is the "parental persuading" approach, bringing your child to the desired outcome with a positive, rather than a confron-tational, approach.

And with your positive approach to begin with, nine times out of 10 you won't need any form of reasoning or persuasion to achieve the desired, appropriate outcome.

The outcome-oriented approach is one way to avoid or prevent arguments.

When your child knows that the outcomes of dis-cussions are positive, without an argument, this will help future discussions. There is a positive cycle with decreased anxiety about future discussions.

And the non-absolute, outcome-oriented approach sets a good example for your child.

YOUR CHILD'S FIRST ANSWER VS. HIS LAST ANSWER

When you ask or tell your child to do something, usually (hopefully) the first answer is "yes" or "okay," or he does what you asked or told him to do. No problem.

If you ask or tell your child to do something and he says "no," don't react and jump to the argument. Do not react to his first or repeated answer, the "no" answer. It's your child's last answer or action, the "yes" answer, the "yes" desired outcome, that's important.

IMPORTANT, MORE IMPORTANT, AND MOST IMPORTANT

In a discussion or a given situation when you have certain information, always consider and prioritize what is important, what is More important and what is Most Important.

There will be times during a discussion when there is a lot of important information and multiple concerns. However, you should always be thinking of what's *most* important for the short term and the long term, and direct the discussion to first focus on the *most* important information and concern.

THE RESTART

Sometimes when the discussion and your child's behavior are deteriorating and your best efforts to avoid or stop an argument, turn things around, and make things better are not successful, the best approach is to offer The Restart.

You saying, "Let's have a restart," interrupts your child's deteriorating behavior, in whatever form it is (escalation, shouting, obscenities, agitation, defiance, etc.) and quickly stops an argument. You may have to offer The Restart more than once.

The Restart gives you the opportunity to refocus the discussion back to the original topic and goal and back to the original positive tone.

The Restart gives your child the opportunity to break his escalating cycle as he works himself up, and regain his composure and self-control.

The discussion directly following The Restart is not the time to remind your son of his recent inappropriate behavior. He knows his behavior was inappropriate, you know his behavior was inappropriate, and he knows that you know his behavior was inappropriate. After all, that's why you're having The Restart. Anytime you need The Restart means that there was inappropriate behavior.

Also, The Restart with a refocus or change in the topic can end a simple disagreement and prevent a disagreement from escalating to an argument.

Safety

The safety of you and your child is always the first priority. Threatening behavior, words or actions, are not the same as your child shouting obscenities or being defiant.

Whenever a discussion is escalating and your child's words or actions give you cause for concern for the safety of you, your child (self-harm), or others, you need to remind him that safety is most important, and you will call 911 if he doesn't stop the threatening behavior. Or just call 911.

GO FOR THE HUG

Sometimes when the discussion and your child's behavior are deteriorating and your best efforts to avoid or stop an argument, turn things around, and make things better are not successful, the best approach is to offer The Hug. (Sound familiar?) Go for The Hug.

You saying, "Let's have a hug," interrupts your child's deteriorating behavior, in whatever form it is (escalation, shouting, obscenities, agitation, defiance, etc.) and is the quick, first step in stopping an argument. The Hug itself stops the argument. You may have to offer The Hug more than once.

For you to offer your child The Hug during an argument when he is shouting and swearing at you may seem difficult and counter intuitive. That makes The Hug even more powerful.

The Hug shows your child that you care much more about him than his inappropriate behavior. And The Hug gives you the opportunity to refocus the discussion back to the original topic and goal and back to the original positive tone.

The Hug gives your child touch, comfort, love, and reassurance. And The Hug gives him the opportunity to take a deep breath, break his escalating cycle as he works himself up, and regain his composure and self-control.

And The Hug is great for you too!

The discussion directly following The Hug is not the time to remind your son of his recent inappropriate behavior. He knows his behavior was inappropriate, you know his behavior was inappropriate, and he knows that you know his behavior was inappropriate. After all, that's why you're having The Hug. Anytime you need The Hug during an argument means that there was inappropriate behavior.

The Hug is the end of an argument and the beginning of peace and moving on.

Please Note: The Restart and The Hug can be combined for extra positive effects. Add a smile for the best feelings for both you and your child.

Safety

Again, the safety of you and your child is always the first priority. Threatening behavior, words or actions, are not the same as your child shouting obscenities or being defiant.

Whenever a discussion is escalating and your child's words or actions give you cause for concern for the safety of you, your child (self-harm), or others, you need to remind him that safety is most important, and you will call 911 if he doesn't stop the threatening behavior. Or just call 911.

MATH – JUST A SUGGESTION ...

You and your child are discussing the subject of math in middle school or high school. This is the classic situation when your child says, "I'm never gonna use this stuff." Here is a suggestion.

You say: "I know. You're right. Unless you are going into engineering or certain other sciences, you are probably not going to use these formulas and equations. That's true." (Your child smiles and says, "That's what I mean.")

You continue: "But the long-term benefit of math is in teaching you how to think and how to think about solving problems. In this case, the problems you are solving are math problems, but the thought process applies to solving problems throughout life. What information or supplies do I need? What information is important? What information do I have that is really not important to solving a particular problem? What is the best way to organize the information and take the appropriate steps to solve the problem? Does the solution to the problem check out and make sense? Math teaches you to think logically and solve all kinds of different problems. In math, there are often different ways to get to the correct solution of a problem. You learn that some ways to solve the problem are easier, more efficient, and better than others. Math is teaching you to think about much more than just the math problems."

Please Note: The points in this chapter, "Content – What You are Saying for Discussions," may also apply to the chapter "Content – What You are Saying Day to Day" and visa-versa.

Chapter Three

MORE PHILOSOPHIES, PRINCIPLES, AND PRACTICES FOR POSITIVE OUTCOMES AND HAPPINESS

HONESTY IS *NOT* THE *BEST* POLICY.... HONESTY IS THE *ONLY* POLICY

You are probably familiar with the saying, "Honesty is the best policy." For generations that famous saying has been helping children learn the importance of being honest, telling the truth, and not lying.

However, there is a problem with the legendary saying. "Honesty is the *best* policy" means there are other "policies" related to telling the truth, including many degrees of being less than completely truthful, but honesty is the best policy among the bunch. "Best" is a relative and comparative term.

When Honesty is the Only Policy, you have a crucial, rock-solid foundation for trust and credibility with your child (and spouse).

You might say that "white lies" are okay to protect your child's feelings. Of course, you never want to hurt your child's feelings. That's when love, tone, and wording make all the difference to protect his feelings.

And with Honesty is the Only Policy, when you, for example, praise your child, he knows, without a doubt, the praise is truthful and meaningful. Trustworthy praise is a relatively minor benefit compared to the importance of trust and your credibility during the many critical discussions you have with your child.

When someone lies to another person, even "white lies," the other person never knows for sure if that someone may be lying again. In addition, once someone is on the lying path, the trail may lead to rationalizations and justifications for increasing the number and consequences of the lies.

In addition to only telling the truth, honesty also applies to your day-to-day interactions and behavior. For example, if you are at a restaurant with your family, order something, it's served, and it's not on the bill, let your server know. For your child, your honest actions every day are worth a thousand talks on honesty. (Of course, your honest actions also apply when you're alone.)

For the lifetime benefit of you and your child, make the saying, "**Honesty is the *Only* Policy.**"

PERSONAL VS. GENERAL PHRASING

Depending on the point you want to make in a sentence and discussion, you can be personal or general.

"You" is personal, "there is" or "there are" are examples of general.

Personal example: If you go to the store after the movies, you're not going to have enough time for the project.

General rephrasing: By going to the store after the movies, there won't be enough time for the project.

Sometimes it's best to speak in general terms and avoid "you." The point is made, and you may avoid an argument.

Personal example: You left the cake in the oven ten minutes too long and now it's overdone.

General rephrasing: The cake was left in the oven ten minutes too long and now it's overdone.

Either way the cake is overdone. But the general phrasing is more diplomatic, avoids assigning the blame, and making things worse.

THE CUMULATIVE EFFECTS OF THE CHILD'S NEGATIVE BEHAVIORS ON THE CURRENT PROBLEM AND YOU

It is helpful for your child to understand that his negative actions over time are not just singular, unrelated events.

His negative behaviors are addressed one at a time, on each occasion, but each incident is also added to an increasing pile of cumulative problems.

Your child thinks and says, "All I did was XYZ. What's so bad?" You think and say, "Yes, XYZ for the twentieth time."

The cumulative, past negative behaviors and consequences provide a context and affects what's said and done for the current problem.

Although it is extremely important to move forward after each individual negative episode is resolved, history is significant. Past negative behaviors are all related to current context.

SPECIAL OCCASIONS AND TRADITIONS... AND MEMORIES

Although well recognized, here is a friendly reminder that the bigger the occasion, the bigger, more important, and longer lasting the memory. This applies to "once in a lifetime" events and annual celebrations.

Whether it's a big, special meal or other celebration, the effort that goes into the meal or event is also extremely important.

Preparing a big meal, such as for Christmas or Thanksgiving, can be stressful. You don't want stress to be the primary feeling for the day or for the memories. Cleaning up as you go along with the cooking and baking will give you more room to work and less stress. The person cleaning has an important role, in addition to the chef and baker.

Cooking, baking, woodworking, gardening, camping, and all your special times and traditions together are supposed to be fun! Enjoy the day! Create a lifetime of positive memories. No arguments.

Remember to take plenty of pictures, which is a positive, stress-decreasing activity. And the photographs will reinforce future memories, as well as decrease stress and increase positive interactions at future special occasions and traditions.

NOT ALWAYS A HAPPY ENDING

Despite all your love and best efforts with your child, there is not always a happy ending. But it's a better ending than would have been without your love and efforts through the years. And you have a clear conscious that you always did the right thing for the right reason. Also, there is the greatest chance for a positive reconciliation and another chance for a happy ending.

SEVERAL SMALL STEPS ARE EASIER THAN ONE BIG STEP

For chores, projects, or your euphemism (e.g., "challenges"), give one chore at a time or a short list of chores. Be specific, which may seem smaller and more manageable than general terms, and avoids misunderstandings (and a potential argument).

For example, say to your child that there are three or four specific things that need to be done and have him pick two. Then he is part of the "decision-making." He feels good to be a part of the process, learns to think through the information and decide, and feels good when the specific things are done, or the project is completed. It's an accomplishment for him!

You should prioritize, and avoid a long, overwhelming list of chores.

AVOID MORE PROBLEMS

Your child does what he is supposed to do or said he would do, when and how he is supposed to do it. That's great.

If your child doesn't do what he is supposed to do that *creates* a problem. But that's different from making that problem worse. You are trying to resolve the problem. Don't make the problem worse or make new problems by arguing about the problem first created by your child.

AVOID ARGUMENTS ABOUT ARGUMENTS

Avoid arguments about previous arguments or words, phrases, or objects used in previous arguments.

You can't go forward when you're going backwards. If you always are going backwards and referring to old arguments during new discussions about new issues, you will always be arguing about past arguments and never go forward. Stress! Avoid stress.

INCREASED QUALITY AND QUANTITY OF LIFE

You have control over the quality and quantity of life, to a point.

Good healthy habits, including decreasing stress, for your family should increase your enjoyment of life and help you live longer. Good health and enjoying time are everything. A serious accident or bad diagnosis will change everything in a second. There are things in life within your control and things that are not in your control.

Avoiding and deceasing arguments and the resulting stress are within your control. You can increase the quality and quantity of life for you and your family.

BLOW OFF STEAM

Some people may say that arguments allow you to "blow off steam," as if that's a necessary or good thing, which it's not.

First, you need to use measures to avoid getting to the point where you think you need to blow off steam (see the rest of this book).

And if you still get to the "blow off steam" point, you need to use alternative methods to starting an argument, which will only create more steam to blow off for you and now another person.

DON'T MAKE WAVES

Some people may say that when you are doing your best to avoid arguments with your child (for all the benefits described in this book), and still accomplish what you need to accomplish with your child, you just "don't want to make waves."

Well, what happens to a ship (you and your family) on the ocean in a storm with waves. The ship struggles to maintain stability and peace. With constant, repeated waves the vessel may sink. The bigger the waves (arguments), the increased risk of the ship sinking. At the very least, increased waves result in a decreased quality of the voyage (daily family life).

With no waves and calm waters for the ship, the vessel is stable, and all the passengers enjoy their voyage together. The ship and passengers get to their destination, the end of each day, week, and month, and achieve their important goals and enjoy those benefits. Smooth sailing is best.

ARGUING SHOWS YOU ARE STRONG. NO.

Arguing shows you're strong? No. You and your position are weak if the way you make your point is by arguing.

When you have the legitimate, correct, right, and best points, you have a discussion, not an argument. You are strong when you have the strong points. You can make legitimate points in a discussion without arguing.

THE PROBLEMS YOU AVOIDED BY NOT ARGUING

When you don't have an argument, you don't know what bad things would have happened with an argument. In other words, you don't know the problems or negative events that you avoided by not arguing.

Therefore, the positive reinforcement for and benefit of avoiding an argument is in enjoying peace and peace of mind, and preventing the "unknown," negative consequnces of an argument.

YOUR CHILD "MAKES THE DECISION"

When you "force" your child to do something that he does not want to do (other than decisions related to your child's safety and health) you lose the opportunity for your child to learn how to think, reason, and decide. Whether he realizes it or not, he is weighing the advantages/pros/positives against the disadvantages/cons/negatives and deciding what to do. That's the decision-making process.

If necessary, one approach is to "encourage" your child to do something, even if it's obvious to you that it is a positive, nice activity. "(The activity) will be fun," "Give it a try," and "This is/will be good because...."

When your child "makes the decision," he has the short-term benefit and positive reinforcement of his decision, enjoying the activity. And less obvious, but more important, he has the long-term benefits of learning how to make decisions, gaining self-confidence and maturity, and becoming independent.

It's important for your child to learn the decision-making process and make relatively easy decisions early in life before he must make more difficult decisions when there are more serious consequences. Later in life, you may not be with him to help him make the right decision.

Life is a long series of good and bad decisions. Help your child early in life make good decisions.

QUESTIONS... ANOTHER WAY TO LOOK AT THE THINGS YOU SAY AND DO

Would you actually *teach* your child to do the things, actions, and behaviors you do, in addition to *lead by example*/daily life and *problem resolution*?

Would you want a dad or mom like you?

Are you repeating the negative behaviors and patterns of your parents?

What could you do differently, that's positive, than you currently do? Then do it.

THE MOST PRECIOUS THING OF ALL: TIME (POSITIVE TIME)

Definition:

It turns out that in Greek mythology, there are two gods associated with the two different kinds of time, which roughly correspond to the Greek words chronos and kairos.

Chronos corresponds to regular cycles, and *kairos* corresponds to progressive flows. Chronos is [quantity], *clock and calendar time*, measurable and predictable, recurring in known cycles. Kairos is *experienced time*, which is nonrecurring and not as predictable, but it flows. Kairos is *quality time*, such as when we talk about having a good time together, finding the right time to say something sensitive, or looking for the right time to make an investment.

Two Kinds of Time | Your Life in Rhythm (wordpress.com)

a: the measured or measurable period during which an action, process, or condition exists or continues: duration

b: a nonspatial continuum that is measured in terms of events which succeed one another from past through present to future

https://www.merriam-webster.com/dictionary/time

Priceless and Precious

Time is a priceless opportunity. Time, as in experienced time and quality time, is more valuable than money, gold, jewels, and any other "valuables."

You know that time is finite, there is a limited amount of time for you and your family to enjoy. However, you don't know *how much* time you have.

It's not only the quantity of time that is important, but the quality of life that you and your family enjoy in whatever amount of time you have. You want your time to be *positive time.*

You should not waste a moment of time, especially wasting precious time with an argument. You and your child (or spouse) can never get back any wasted time.

You have a limited ability to control the amount of time you have. Bad genes and bad luck can reduce your quantity of time.

You have a nearly unlimited ability to control the enjoyment of the priceless time you and your family spend together. And that is based on your positive priorities.

YOUR CHILD GOES ABOUT IT THE RIGHT WAY

When your child wants to do something that he knows you may not entirely approve of, but something can be worked out, it's important that he go about making plans the right way.

The wrong way example: Your child knows when he goes to the mall, he must be home by 6:00. But your child defiantly says, "I'm going to the mall with John until 7." Or worse: Your child defiantly says, "I'm going to the mall. I'll be back later."

Don't react or, worse, overreact. That's the start of an argument. Instead, nicely remind your child that's the wrong way to go about making plans, ask him questions to get more information, and resolve the situation peacefully.

The right way example: Your child pleasantly and maybe a little tentatively, says, "I know that when I go to the mall, I'm supposed to be home by 6:00. But I haven't seen John in a few weeks, and we'd like to stay until 7. Is that okay? I'm trying to go about making plans the right way."

When your child goes about making plans the right way, that should be acknowledged, and he should be given credit for it. You should try to work something out. By working something out, either the 7:00 requested time or a 6:30 compromise, your child is "rewarded" for going about making plans the right way.

Your child knows you will try to accommodate a reasonable request when he goes about it the right way. And he knows that if you say no, there's a good reason.

When your child learns to go about something, like making plans, the right way, that's another way to prevent arguments.

HOW CAN WE? VS. WE CAN'T

It's important to teach your child that positive questioning and positive thinking creates positive outcomes.

Turn the phrase "I/we can't do this" into "How can I/we do this?"

The more significant and/or complicated the plan, proposal, event, occasion, task, project, or job, the more effort may be needed to turn "Can't" into "Can." But the extra thought, time, and effort are well worth it.

Whenever your child says, "I can't do XYZ because ....," you say, "Wait a minute, let's think, how can we do XYZ?"

Eventually, your child will be changing the "Can't" into "Can" on his own.

Of course, this approach doesn't work when it's obvious that Can't really, realistically means Can't.

(This is how Obi Wan Kenobi started his Jedi Mind Tricks!)

ALWAYS DO THE RIGHT THING FOR THE RIGHT REASON

One of the most critical philosophies, turned into a principle, is Always Do the Right Thing for The Right Reason. This is a principle, your mindset, not something you have to keep reminding yourself about.

Each day you have a long series of decisions to make. Most are straight forward. What do you have for breakfast? What clothes do you wear to work? But some decisions, especially certain decisions relating to your child, are more complex.

For example, you are planning to take your child out for a surprise, special lunch.

Right thing: Both you and your child enjoy a surprise, special lunch.

Right reason: To have a special time together and create wonderful memories for you and your child.

. . .

Right thing: Both you and your child enjoy a surprise, special lunch.

Wrong reason: You may start out with good intentions, but the next time he doesn't do his chores you remind him about you taking him for a "special" lunch. Your special time together is contingent on your child doing something, after the event. You turn something positive into something negative.

. . .

Wrong thing: You plan a surprise, special lunch, and you tell your child about it, but when he doesn't do his chores that morning, you say you're not going to take him for the special lunch.

Wrong reason: Your original motivation for the surprise, special lunch is contingent on your child doing something. You turn something positive into something negative.

Always Doing the Right Thing for The Right Reason gives you peace of mind. You never have to second guess about anything you do for your child and in life. And if something doesn't work out, you have a clear conscience.

Always Do the Right Thing for The Right Reason is a saying you should teach your child, as well as teach by example.

YOU'RE HUMAN

You always do your best when you interact with your child and others throughout the day. But there will be times when, despite your best efforts, you are less than perfect. That's because you're human. It's difficult to always be perfect.

If you are disappointed with, and possibly regret, your actions, that shows you recognize that you had a problem and you care about it. Then you can acknowledge your actions and the problem, apologize, if appropriate, and learn from your mistakes. Learning from a difficult episode helps you develop ways to prevent future difficult episodes.

After you have addressed your imperfect actions and learned from the episode, don't dwell on it. It's important to move on.

The positive way you handle less-than-perfect actions will set a positive example for your child.

REALITY REFOCUS PHRASES: IT DOESN'T MATTER, NO BIG DEAL, IT'S OKAY ...

Sometimes the smallest phrases have the largest effect.

Many disagreements, misunderstandings, or conflicts can be "resolved," stopped, and refocused onto another topic with a Reality Refocus Phrase.

Reality Refocus Phrases: "It doesn't matter," "No big deal," "It's okay," "Let it go," "Easy does it," "It's not important," "Don't worry," "No problem," and "It's fine."

The magic phrases can be combined for added effect and reassurance, such as "It's okay. No problem." Or "It doesn't matter. It's fine."

It's crucial to recognize when a disagreement is not significant (and most disagreements are not significant); may be unnecessarily escalating, perhaps to an argument; and you have the power to quickly put an end to the disagreement with two or three words. The same is true for misunderstandings or minor conflicts. Just pick the appropriate Reality Refocus Phrase that fits the discussion.

The phrase will help your child realize it really doesn't matter or be reassured there really isn't a problem, and move on with you to another topic.

SINCERELY SORRY

If your child does something bad, wrong, or inappropriate, the first step for him to make things better is for him to recognize that his behavior was bad.

Your child just saying, "I'm sorry," may be sufficient, especially with the appropriate tone of voice and body language.

If he just says, "I'm sorry," when appropriate, you may say, "Sorry for what?" Not that you are doubting his sincerity, but to help him think, and maybe talk, about what he did wrong. This can help get to the "why" in addition to the "what" he did.

When your child does something bad, realizes it (or you tell him it's wrong), and says he is sorry, your child learns a valuable lesson. You help him understand the right alternative.

When he says, "I'm sorry," *don't* say, "No, you're not sorry." First, you are calling him a liar. And second, you are starting an argument. You say, "No, you're not sorry." He says, "Yes, I am sorry." You say, "No, you're Not." He says, "Yes, I Am." ... "No, You're Not." "Yes, I Am!" At this point, what your child did wrong, his apology, and learning from his actions is lost.

If you had done something wrong, been sincerely sorry, and said, "I'm sorry for XYZ," and the other person said, "No you're not sorry," how would *you* feel?

The Exception

Hopefully not for you, but there are times when a child or young adult absolutely knows in advance something he does is very wrong, deliberately does it, there are serious negative outcomes, and he is caught. That's far more serious than the day-to-day poor judgment or mistakes discussed above.

Chapter Four

CONTENT – WHAT YOU ARE SAYING DAY TO DAY

PLEASE AND THANK YOU

"Please" and "thank you" are two simple terms that add the most positive tone to any interaction, statement, or conversation every day.

Whenever you ask your child to do something, just add "please," either at the beginning, middle, or end of the sentence. You're not emphasizing the "please" or making a big deal of the word. "Please" becomes part of speaking.

And you can do the same when speaking with people on the phone or outside the house. Saying "please" and "thank you" to other people sets a great example for your child.

"Please" doesn't have to be an exceptional, "magic word." "Please" is more magical when it is used regularly. Small word, big difference.

"Thank you" works very well together with "please."

In addition, a simple "thank you" is perfect when you need a polite acknowledgement of something that is obvious, or you already know. For example, when you are driving and your child says, "The store is up here on the left." You can either say, "Yes, I can see it." Or "Yes, I know." Or simply a nice "Thank you." Which phrase will make your child feel best and most helpful?

SUFFIXES CAN BE MORE EFFECTIVE THAN ABSOLUTES

The suffixes "-er" and "-est" are powerful and can prevent an escalation from a discussion to an argument.

For instance, in a discussion, your child is raising his voice (or yelling) ...

First scenario: You: "Stop raising your voice." Him: "I'm not raising my voice!" You: You Are Raising Your Voice." Him: No, I'm Not Raising My Voice!!" You: "Yes, You Are Raising Your Voice!" Him: "No, I'm NOT Raising My Voice!!!"

Alternative: Calmly and quietly say, "Please speak softer." .... Repeat if needed. If necessary: "Please speak your softest." Or "Please be quieter." And "Please be your quietest." May repeat.

HELP DIRECT THE LISTENER'S BRAIN AND THOUGHTS

When thinking and processing information, the human brain works extremely fast, but it does not always know which way to take a thought. That's why it is important to set the right course by starting a sentence or new topic with the key word or phrase.

Introduce the subject of the sentence (or paragraph) with the subject of the sentence (or paragraph) up front to let the listener's brain know what you are talking about and where you are going. This approach makes a big difference to improve clarity, decrease misunderstandings, and prevent arguments.

Let your child know what you are going to be talking about, especially when you are changing subjects, or your child may think you have bad news.

First example: "I spoke with your school principal today. He is very pleased with the progress you're making with your math homework."

Correct alternative: "Good news about your math homework. I spoke with your school principal today and he very pleased with your progress."

Second example: "You know that, unfortunately, Aunt Mary has been very sick and needed an operation. The operation was a success, and she is doing great!

Correct alternative: "Aunt Mary is doing great! She was very sick, but she had the operation, and it was a success.

When you have a new topic or a change in topic, you can always say, "On the subject of (fill in the blank)" and continue from there. "On the subject of..." is a perfect way to transition from a completed topic to introduce a new topic.

SIMPLE ANSWERS AND QUESTIONS WITHOUT NEGATIVE ADDITIONS

When your child asks a simple question, provide a simple answer. If the question is a "yes or no" question, answer with a "yes" or a "no," without any negative comments.

This is especially important when there was a recent problem; don't tie the old problem to his new question. Just nicely say "yes" or "no," or provide the answer to the question, with a smile.

When there is not a negative comment with your answers, you will get a lot more questions from your child. And questions and interactions with your child are a positive thing.

When asking your child a question or asking him to do something, if there is no response just nicely repeat the question, request, or comment, without a negative comment (such as, "I'm talking to you!").

CONJUNCTIONS CAN BE GOOD OR BAD

Definition

A word such as "and," "but," "while," or "although" that connects words, phrases, and clauses in a sentence.

https://dictionary.cambridge.org/us/dictionary/ english/conjunction

Words [that] function as connectors between words, phrases, clauses, or sentences, as *and*, *but*, *however*.

Conjunction Definition & Meaning | Dictionary.com

Conjunctions Can Set the Tone; Positive or Negative.

But

The conjunction "but" is typically good and is useful to give a positive alternative for your child.

Example: We can't go to the store, but we can go to the park. (A positive tone of voice helps.)

Or

The conjunction "or" (or "or else") is generally bad, especially with the words "not" or "can't," and easily taken as a threat by your child, unless a positive alternative is offered.

Negative example: You need to pick up your room now or you can't go to the show!

Positive rephrasing: After you pick up your room you can go to the show.

So

The conjunction "so" can be bad or good.

Negative example: You didn't pick up your room, so you can't go to the show. (Unfortunately, that's past tense.)

Positive rephrasing: Please pick up your room, so you can go to the show.

If

The conjunction "If" (as in if/then) can be positive or negative.

Negative example: If you don't pick up your room, then you can't go to the show.

Positive rephrasing: If you pick up your room, then you can go to the show.

Threat vs. Reward

You may think the above two sentences are similar. But the negative if/then phrasing is in the form of a threat. When you use a negative if/then statement, it can/will be felt by your child to be a threat. You are taking something away from him.

The positive if/then phrasing is in the form of a reward.

Just about any negative phrase can be rephrased or reworded to a positive phrase, when using conjunctions and in general.

Please note: The points in this chapter, "Content – What You are Saying Day to Day," may also apply to the chapter "Content – What You are Saying for Discussions," and visa-versa.

CONCLUSION

The most important point about the conclusion of this book is that you can achieve the goals and enjoy the benefits discussed in this book. In fact, you are the most important person in achieving these goals and enjoying the benefits of a family with peace, no arguments, and happiness.

To highlight and review the most (but not the only) essential points, we have ...

THE TOP TWENTY-FIVE TAKEAWAYS (IN ORDER OF PAGE NUMBERS)

1. It's Not personal. (page 7)
2. Be Slow to Anger, and Quick to Recovery. (page 11)
3. It's all about The Positive Memories. (pages 16, 18)
4. Save Precious Time. (pages 17, 74)
5. Of Body Language, Distance, Setting, Tone, and Volume, the three most important factors for a positive outcome to a discussion with your child, or anything you say to your child, are Tone, Tone, and Tone...... and Tone. (page 21)

6. Always be Positive in Tone; Never Negative. (page 21)
7. If your Child Raises his Voice, Lower your Voice. (page 31)
8. Your child's "Lying Expression" speaks louder than his words. (page 38)
9. Observe Changes and Trends in body language. (page 39)
10. Recognizing your child's Triggers, known and unknown, is critical. (page 40)
11. Keep your Mouth Closed and Listen. (page 44)
12. When information is important, Say it's important. (page 47)
13. Do Not use Derogatory or Demeaning Words, they become the focus of the discussion. (page 49)
14. Focus on one topic/priority at a time. (page 50)
15. Be Outcome Oriented. (page 56)
16. What's important, More important, and Most Important. (page 57)
17. Stop an argument with The Restart; Go for the Hug. (page 58)
18. Honesty is not the best policy. Honesty is the only policy. (page 63)
19. Your child's past behaviors are not necessarily prelude; his past behaviors are Context. (page 66)

20. Always move Forward; Never go Backward. (page 69)
21. Don't React and definitely Don't Overreact. (page 75)
22. Always do the Right Thing for the Right Reason. (page 77)
23. It doesn't matter. Don't worry. It's okay. No big deal. No problem. Let it go. Easy does it. (page 80)
24. Say Please and Thank You. (page 83)
25. Help direct your child's (the listener's) brain. (page 85)

Alone, any one of the essential points can make a positive difference for you, your children, and family. Together, these points, along with the other topics in this book, can make a major, positive difference in the quality of your family's daily life.

The earlier you start in your child's life, the greater the opportunity to have more positive outcomes, happiness, and wonderful memories. But.... It's never too late.

As is often the case, the conclusion is also the beginning. The beginning of making a positive difference for you, your children, and family. Start today.

INDEX